DISCARD

W9-CLL-327

JOANNA COLE

A Horse's Body

PHOTOGRAPHS BY JEROME WEXLER

William Morrow and Company
New York 1981

J
599.72
C

Text copyright © 1981 by Joanna Cole
Photographs copyright © 1981 by Jerome Wexler

All rights reserved. No part of this book may be reproduced or
utilized in any form or by any means, electronic or mechanical,
including photocopying, recording or by any information
storage and retrieval system, without permission in writing from
the Publisher. Inquiries should be addressed to William Morrow
and Company, Inc., 105 Madison Ave., New York, N.Y. 10016.

Design by Cynthia Basil.

Printed in the United States of America.
1 2 3 4 5 6 7 8 9 10

Library of Congress Cataloging in Publication Data

Cole, Joanna. A horse's body.

   Summary: An introduction to the horse, its habits, anatomy,
physiology, and evolution.
1. Horses—Juvenile literature. [1. Horses]
I. Wexler, Jerome. II. Title.
SF302.C64   599.72′5   80-28147
ISBN 0-688-00362-1   ISBN 0-688-00363-X (lib. bdg.)

The author thanks
Steven Shaff, D.V.M.,
for his very helpful reading
of the manuscript.
The photographer thanks
George Simpson, Jr.,
owner of Skylinvue Farm,
Wallingford, Connecticut,
Lydia Frein, and Annalisa Hall
for their assistance
with the photographs.

For Tanya and Joshua Birenbaum

When you look at a horse, you see a large beautiful animal with long legs, hard hoofs, and a big barrel chest.

The horse is an animal that is perfectly suited for running over flat grasslands. Its body seems to have been designed especially to run.

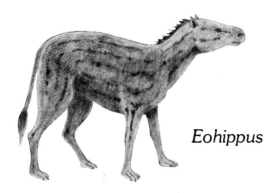

Eohippus

The horses of today are all descended from one ancestor. This ancestor was a forest-dwelling animal that lived fifty million years ago. It was not a large animal with long legs and hoofs. Instead, it was small—about the size of a fox—and it had several toes on each foot.

Because it is the ancestor of the horse, it is named *Eohippus*, which means "dawn horse" in Greek.

Over millions of years, new kinds of horses came into being. Scientists think that horses evolved as they did because the environment around them changed.

Forests slowly changed into grassy plains. As land became more open, early horses needed to run fast to escape from enemies. Those horses that were larger and had longer legs were the ones that stayed alive.

THE EVOLUTION OF THE HORSE

Eohippus
50 million years ago

Mesohippus
35-30 million years ago

Merychippus
25-20 million years ago

Pliohippus
5-2 million years ago

Equus
2 million years ago

The horse's long legs are made up of elongated, or stretched out, leg bones. The part of the leg that you can see is actually made of only the shin, foot, and toe bones. But these bones are much longer than the same ones in other animals. As you can see in the picture, the parts of the leg that would correspond to the human thigh and hip are concealed within the body of the horse.

hip

thigh

knee

shin

ankle

elongated foot bones

elongated toe bones

shoulder

elbow

wrist

elongated foot bones

elongated toe bones

9

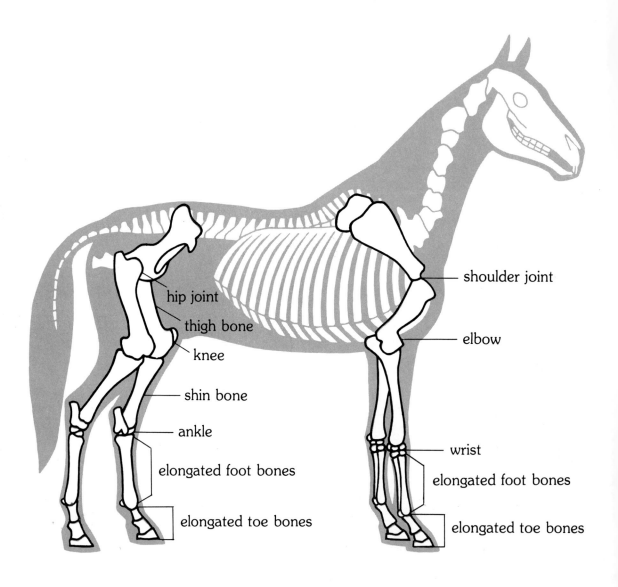

hip joint

thigh bone

knee

shin bone

ankle

elongated foot bones

elongated toe bones

shoulder joint

elbow

wrist

elongated foot bones

elongated toe bones

10

When the horse runs, its stiff spine does not move. Only its legs are in motion. They are moved like levers by powerful muscles at the top of each limb. This arrangement gives the horse a very long stride.

By comparison, the cheetah gains a long stride because of its flexible spine. The cheetah can run faster than the horse for short sprints, but its method of running uses more energy. The cheetah tires after 500 yards, while a horse can run without stopping for four miles.

A horse's legs are built so that it can stand with hardly any effort. Its joints will stay in place without using muscle power. For this reason, a horse can doze easily while standing up.

When a horse sleeps more soundly, however, it must lie down. Then the horse's stiff spine makes it very hard to get up and down.

13

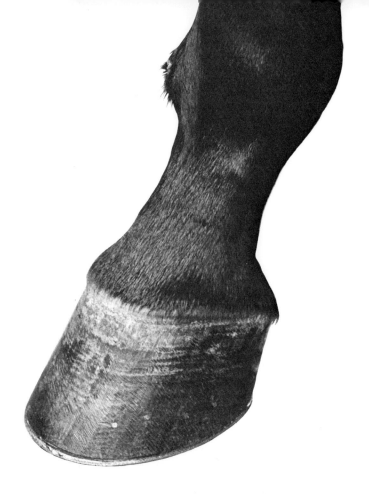

Like its legs, a horse's feet are also perfect for running over flat land. Although prehistoric horses had several toes, the foot of a modern horse is actually an enlarged single toe, which is covered with a tough hoof.

On the outside of the hoof is a covering called the hoof wall. This wall grows downward from top to bottom, so it is always being replaced like a fingernail. The hoof wall is strong enough to hold up most of the horse's weight.

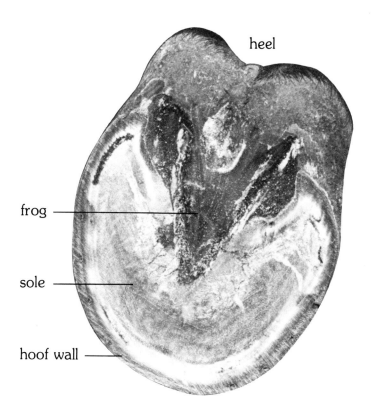

heel

frog

sole

hoof wall

When the horse runs, there may be 2,000 pounds of pressure on a single hoof and leg. To help handle this pressure, the hoof acts as a natural shock absorber.

The heel touches the ground first and pushes on the wedge-shaped frog of the foot. Then the frog pushes on the rubbery sole and makes it expand. This expansion compresses the blood in the foot's blood vessels, which then act like cushions.

Each time the hoof strikes the ground, it expands. And each time it is lifted from the ground, it returns to its normal shape.

A blacksmith makes
each shoe out of molten steel
to fit the hoof exactly.

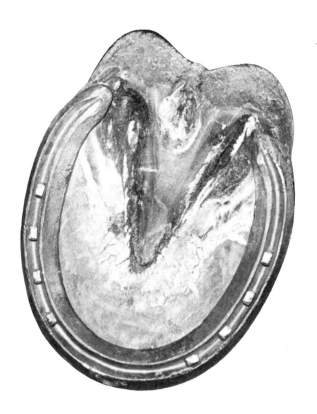

Bare hoofs are tough enough for a wild horse that lives on a grassy plain. But the hoofs of a riding horse get more wear than those of a wild horse.

A riding horse has to carry a heavy person on its back. It may have to run on hard roads. And it often has to run for longer periods than it would in nature. Therefore, many horses need metal shoes to keep their hoofs from getting too worn down.

The shoes are put on with nails, but they don't hurt the horse because the nails are driven into a part of the hoof wall that has no feeling.

A four-footed animal usually walks by lifting one foot at a time. So a slow-walking horse can almost never topple over, because it is held up at all times by three feet.

19

When the horse walks faster or when it trots, it lifts the next foot before the first one touches the ground. So there are only two feet on the ground at a time— one forefoot and the hind foot on the opposite side. In a trot, the horse loses some stability but gains speed.

As the horse moves even faster, at a canter or a gallop, usually only one foot touches the ground at a time. When the horse is moving at top speed, no feet touch the ground in mid stride.

23

To run for long distances at high speeds, a horse needs a lot of oxygen. A horse's lungs are very large and can take in large amounts of air.

The heart is also extra big, so it can pump the oxygen-rich blood to all parts of the body. The average weight of a horse's heart is nine pounds, and the heart of one very fast race-horse weighed fourteen pounds. By comparison, the heart of a human being weighs less than one pound.

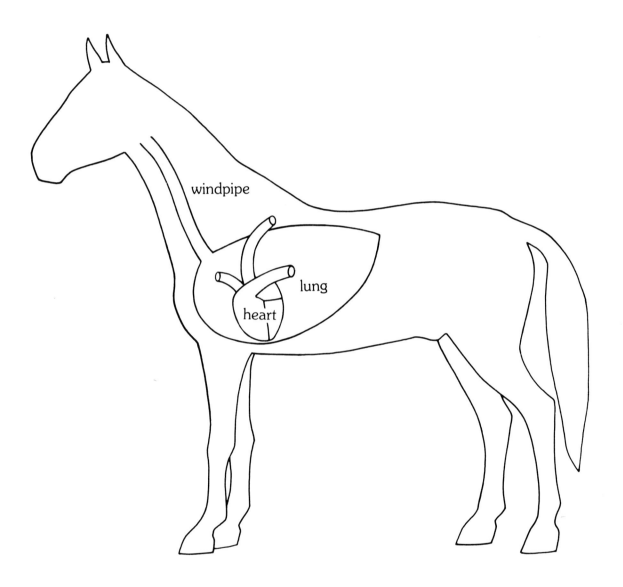

windpipe

lung

heart

When a horse gallops, its body temperature goes up so fast and so high that it would die if it did not have a rapid way of cooling off. Fortunately, it can do so by sweating.

Most furred animals do not sweat; they cool themselves by panting. Sweating uses more water than panting, but it cools the body more quickly.

Sweating would not be a good way to cool an animal with long, thick fur. However, it does work well for the horse, which has a sleek hide.

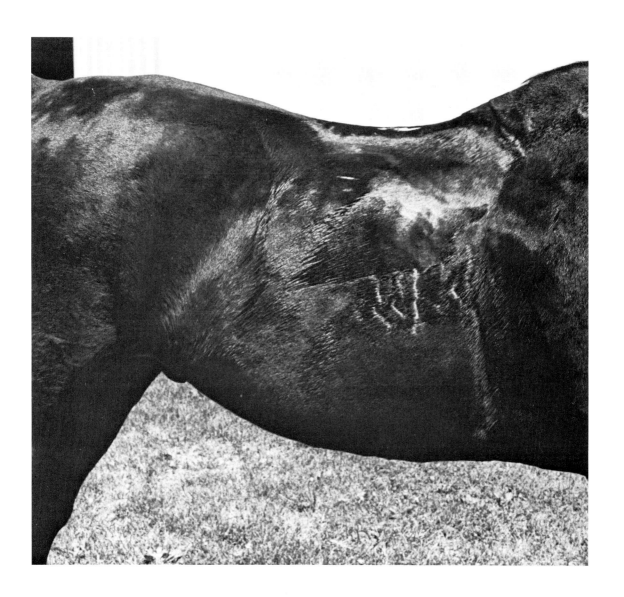

The horse's evolution has determined not only how it runs but also how it eats. The horse's ancestor, *Eohippus*, was probably a leaf eater that browsed off low shrubs. But today's horse, which developed on the plains, is a grass eater. Grasses are harder to eat and digest than other plants. Therefore, the horse has a special digestive system to deal with grass.

Grasses contain more tough fibers than leaves. So grazing animals need sharper and stronger teeth than browsers.

The horse's sharp front teeth are used for biting off grass. The large rear teeth, or molars, grind it up.

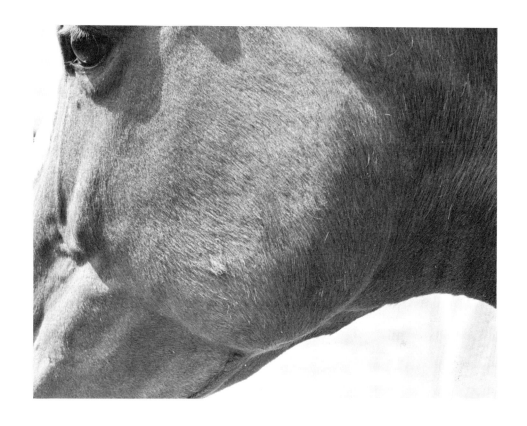

It takes about twenty minutes for a horse to chew one pound of hay—or dried grass—and an average horse might eat from twenty to thirty pounds of hay a day. Because of all this chewing, horses need very large jaw muscles, which you can see in the picture.

Because grass is so hard to digest, some grazing animals, like cows and sheep, have special four-part stomachs and spend many hours each day chewing their cud. Horses, however, are not cud chewers and have a simple stomach like a human being's.

They do have a special digestive tract, though, that is over 100 feet long. One part of the intestine, called the "caecum," contains bacteria that break down the tough fibers in the grass.

The digestive tract of the horse is longer than that of other animals its size. But the stomach is smaller. For this reason, a horse cannot eat all the food it needs in a single meal and must be fed several times a day.

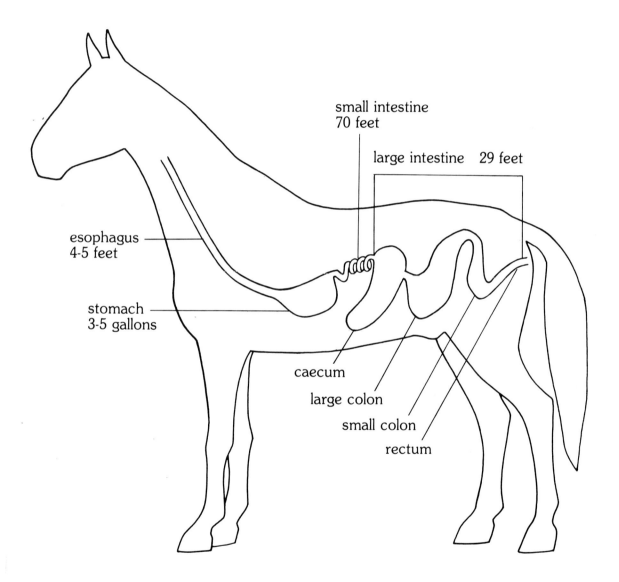

small intestine
70 feet

large intestine   29 feet

esophagus
4-5 feet

stomach
3-5 gallons

caecum

large colon

small colon

rectum

33

In nature, a horse spends at least half the day with its head down, eating grass. But it still can detect predators approaching because it can see in almost a full circle. With its eyes placed high on the sides of its face, the horse can see almost everything except an object close to the center of its forehead.

Although horses have such a wide range of vision, they do not usually see things very sharply. Instead, they notice movement, and they are ready to run at the first hint of danger. To prevent nervousness, a horse owner may put blinders on the horse to keep it from seeing objects behind it.

The human eye brings objects into sharp focus by changing the shape of the lens. A horse's eyes focus quite differently—by moving the angle of the head. That is why horses often raise and lower their heads. This action may seem like nervousness, but actually the horse is only trying to focus its eyes.

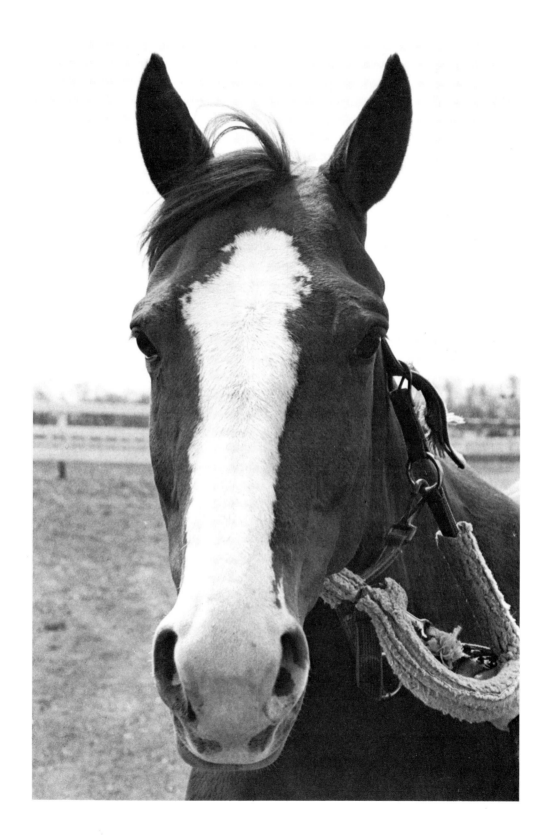

A horse can hear sounds several miles away, and it can hear not only with its ears but also through its legs. Vibrations from the ground travel up the leg bones, so a horse can detect something large moving a quarter of a mile away.

Because they can hear sounds so far away, horses get nervous when a storm is coming long before human ears can hear it. For this reason, some people have thought horses could "predict" the weather through ESP.

Horses usually keep their ears facing front, but they can turn the ears a full 180 degrees. Because of these swivel ears, they can pinpoint any sound exactly.

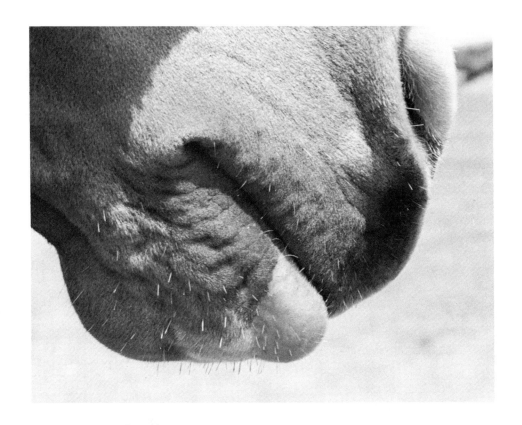

The horse's velvet-soft muzzle is the center of its sense of touch. The muzzle is covered with bristles, which are extra-sensitive, because each one is connected to a cluster of nerves at its root. A horse can tell a lot about the size and position of its food through these hairs.

By means of the sense of touch in its skin, a horse can sometimes tell what a human rider wants even before the rider gives the signal. The reason is that the person's muscles make small movements before giving the signal, movements that he is not aware of. Through its skin, the horse can feel these tiny muscle twitches, and a rider sometimes gets the feeling that the horse can read his mind.

Horses can tell a lot about the world with their sense of smell. They use smell to identify other horses. When two horses meet each other, they greet by blowing into one another's nostrils.

Horses are frightened by the smell of a dead animal. Even the smell of a tiny dead mouse will scare a horse. This reaction is probably a way of protecting the herd against a predator that might still be near its kill.

A special sense of smell is used mainly by stallions, or male horses. When a stallion detects a female, he pulls up his lip, closes his jaws, and wrinkles his nostrils.

Scientists call this odd grimace "flehmen". They believe that "flehmen" allows the odor of the female horse to reach a special smell organ in the roof of the stallion's mouth.

A stallion can tell whether a mare is ready to mate even if she is a half a mile away.

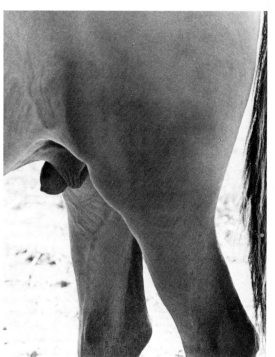

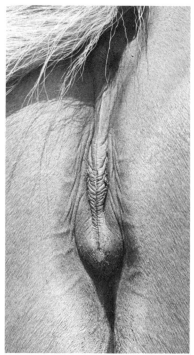

MALE:
OUTSIDE SEX ORGANS

FEMALE:
OUTSIDE SEX ORGANS

   To survive as a species, horses must bear young. Like other mammals, they mate, and the male's sperm joins with the ovum, or egg cell, in the female.

   Then the unborn baby horse, or foal, grows in the mare's womb for about eleven months.

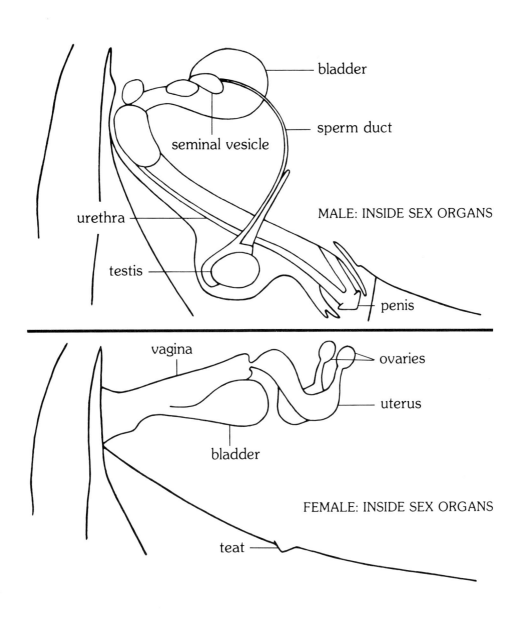

bladder

sperm duct

seminal vesicle

MALE: INSIDE SEX ORGANS

urethra

testis

penis

vagina

ovaries

uterus

bladder

FEMALE: INSIDE SEX ORGANS

teat

43

As soon as it comes into the world, a foal shows that it was born to be a plains dweller. In a very short time, it can stand and suck milk from its mother's teats. Within an hour or two, it can run after the mare.

The foal's early ability to stand and run is another adaptation of horses to life on the plains. Newborns that could not follow the herd would be left behind and would not survive.

Whether the foal is destined to become a saddle horse, a racehorse, or even a workhorse, it will always have the special body of an animal that was born to run.

About the Author

Born in Newark, New Jersey, Joanna Cole grew up in East Orange. After attending the University of Massachusetts and Indiana University, she earned a B.A. degree in psychology at the City College of New York. Later she took graduate courses in elementary education at New York University and served for one year in a Brooklyn elementary school as a librarian. Author of many science books for the youngest reader, Mrs. Cole now lives in New York City with her husband and daughter.

About the Photographer

Jerome Wexler was born in New York City, where he attended Pratt Institute. Later he studied at the University of Connecticut. His interest in photography started when he was in the ninth grade. After service in World War II, he worked for the State Department in Europe as a photographer. Returning to the United States, he specialized in photographing farming techniques, and the pictures he made have been published throughout the world. Since then he has illustrated a number of children's books with his photographs of plants and animals.

At present, Mr. Wexler lives in Wallingford, Connecticut.